Most Phenomenal Modern Buildings

Cathy Marks Krpan

Series Editor
Jeffrey D. Wilhelm

Much thought, debate, and research went into choosing and ranking the 10 items in each book in this series. We realize that everyone has his or her own opinion of what is most significant, revolutionary, amazing, deadly, and so on. As you read, you may agree with our choices, or you may be surprised — and that's the way it should be!

an imprint of

SCHOLASTIC

www.scholastic.com/librarypublishing

A Rubicon book published in association with Scholastic Inc.

Associate Publishers: Kim Koh, Miriam Bardwich
Project Editor: Amy Land
Editorial Assistant: Nikki Yeh
Creative Director: Jennifer Drew
Project Manager/Designer: Jeanette MacLean
Graphic Designer: Jeanette MacLean

The publisher gratefully acknowledges the following for permission to reprint copyrighted material in this book.

Every reasonable effort has been made to trace the owners of copyrighted material and to make due acknowledgment. Any errors or omissions drawn to our attention will be gladly rectified in future editions.

"A Palace of Rock" (excerpt) by Nicholas Jennings. From *Maclean's* magazine, September 18, 1995. Reprinted with permission.

"Gehry's First Hotel Sparkles" (excerpt from "Gehry's First Hotel Sparkles in Rioja Alavesa") by Susan Spano. From the *Los Angeles Times*, March 1, 2007. Reprinted with permission.

"Egypt Opens New Library of Alexandria" (excerpt) by Chad Cohen. From *National Geographic Today*, October 16, 2002. Reprinted with permission.

Cover image: La Grande Arche–Getty Images/Stone/Doug Armand

Library and Archives Canada Cataloguing in Publication

Krpan, Cathy Marks
The 10 most phenomenal modern buildings / Cathy Marks Krpan.

Includes index.
ISBN: 978-1-55448-496-6

1. Readers (Elementary). 2. Readers—Architecture, Modern.
I. Title. II. Title: Ten most phenomenal modern buildings.

PE1117.K773 2007 428.6 C2007-906869-3

1 2 3 4 5 6 7 8 9 10 10 17 16 15 14 13 12 11 10 09 08

Printed in Singapore

Contents

Form and Function

American architect Louis Sullivan (1856 – 1924) is regarded as the creator of the skyscraper. He believed that when designing buildings, "form ever follows function." A building cannot just look good — it must first meet the needs of the people using it.

Designing a phenomenal building involves creativity and teamwork. Architects design buildings that are visually appealing and fulfill the purpose for which they are built. After sketching out their ideas, architects work with engineers to make sure that the design can be converted into a safe, strong building. Together, they also decide on the materials to use for the building. Sometimes, they have to invent new materials for the structures! Lately, the trend has been to use materials that are also environmentally friendly.

ILLUSTRATIONS BY BRANDON KÖPKE

In this book, we present what we think are the 10 most phenomenal modern buildings. We selected and ranked them using the following criteria:

form — the beauty and originality of the design;
function — the effective use of the interior spaces;
materials — the efficient and creative use of materials; and
construction — the engineering required to build the structure.

As you read about these buildings, think like an architect and ask yourself:

What makes a building phenomenal?

10 ROCK AND ROLL HA

Perched on the edge of Lake Erie, the Rock and Roll Hall of Fame and Museum looks like something from a fantasy movie.

LL OF FAME AND MUSEUM

ARCHITECT: I. M. Pei, born 1917

FUNCTION: Museum and hall of fame

LOCATION: Cleveland, Ohio

DATE COMPLETED: 1995

The Rock and Roll Hall of Fame and Museum celebrates everything that has to do with rock and roll music. Architect I. M. Pei played with different geometric shapes to create a building that looks as lively as the music industry it celebrates.

A block-shaped tower that stands 160 feet tall soars from the water. A 125-seat theater is cantilevered from this tower, 59 feet above the water. Beside the tower, a cylindrical drum sits atop a slender column. This circular exhibition hall looks like a stack of records on a turntable. At the front of the building, a huge glass pyramid ties all of these shapes together.

One whole floor of the building is devoted to inductees to the hall of fame. The museum houses a large collection of rock and roll memorabilia, from old microphones and recording equipment to clothing and cars belonging to rock and roll stars such as Elvis Presley and the Beatles. The museum's interactive exhibits, films, videos, and priceless artifacts offer visitors the actual sights and sounds of rock and roll — its history, the scene today, and what is to come. From the architecture to what's inside, the Rock and Roll Hall of Fame and Museum is one rockin' building!

---

cantilevered: *attached to and jutting out from a supporting structure*
inductees: *people chosen to be honored*
memorabilia: *objects treasured for their connection to memorable events; souvenirs*

Find out who are some of the most recent inductees into the Rock and Roll Hall of Fame. Do you think they deserve the honor? Why?

ROCK AND ROLL HALL OF FAME AND MUSEUM

LOOKING GOOD!

Architect I. M. Pei created a museum with a unique design, linking different geometric shapes with his signature feature — a glass pyramid. He also made excellent use of the interior spaces — from well-lit walkways and open balconies to exhibition halls, theaters, and a museum store. To save space and to also create a climate-controlled environment for the exhibits, he designed the museum so that a large part of it would be in the basement.

signature: *distinguishing style of an individual*

What do you think is meant by someone's "signature feature"? Can you think of an example of the signature feature of your favorite musician, writer, or artist?

Cars from U2's Zoo TV Tour hang from the ceiling in the lobby of The Rock and Roll Hall of Fame and Museum.

BRICKS AND MORE

Architect I. M. Pei used concrete for the walls and aluminum for the ceilings. The balcony railings were crafted out of stainless steel and glass. The pyramid was also built out of glass. The glass has a special metal coating that allows the sun to shine through without heating up the inside of the museum. This is very important, as some of the priceless memorabilia could be damaged by heat.

ARCHITECT

Architect I. M. Pei has designed over 50 buildings around the world, from low-income housing to grand cultural and commercial buildings. In 1983, Pei was awarded the Pritzker Prize, the most prestigious award in architecture. In the citation, the jury said: "I. M. Pei has given this century some of its most beautiful interior spaces and exterior forms. … His versatility and skill in the uses of materials approach the level of poetry."

citation: *speech recognizing someone's achievements*
versatility: *ability to change frequently*

Do some research. Find out the skills and accomplishments the award jury looks for when they select a winner for the Pritzker Prize. What do you think is meant by the last sentence of the jury's citation for Pei's work?

Quick Fact

This museum has the largest Elvis Presley exhibition outside of Memphis, Tennessee. Some of the Rock and Roll Hall of Fame and Museum's Elvis memorabilia include his army uniform and old crayon box.

The Expert Says...

"This building is a stunning structure, a marvel of museum architecture, and a major accomplishment for both the architect and the history of architecture …"

— Dr. Lori Verderame, museum curator

marvel: *wonder*

10 9 8 7 6

A PALACE OF ROCK

A magazine article from *Maclean's* ★ By Nicholas Jennings, September 18, 1995

Judging by the scores of fans who flooded into the facility during its ... weekend opening — an estimated 8,000 on the first day — the Rock and Roll Hall of Fame and Museum is now a resounding success. Visitors can feast on more than 3,500 items, ranging from posters, album jackets, and handwritten lyric sheets, to movies and interactive exhibits that play requested songs and videos. ...

The actual Hall of Fame is housed on the top floor. ... To get there, visitors climb a long, spiral staircase to reach a darkened room honoring the inductees. ... Images of such legends as Buddy Holly and Bob Marley dissolve on tiny video screens like ghosts, while their signatures, etched on backlit glass plaques, seem to float in the [air]. After the musical cacophony and video chaos downstairs, the Hall of Fame is a welcome sanctuary.

For the Hall of Fame's creators, the museum was a [fantastic plan] that almost never materialized. Founders Jann Wenner, editor of *Rolling Stone*, and Ahmet Ertegun, president of Atlantic Records, steered the project through three directors and one site change before the groundbreaking two years ago. Cleveland was chosen over Memphis and New York after residents collected 600,000 signatures and local businesses raised $87 million. ...

resounding: *big*
etched: *carved*
cacophony: *jarring sounds*

Take Note

The Rock and Roll Hall of Fame and Museum takes the #10 spot. It combines a unique design with excellent use of interior spaces that serve many purposes, from photographs to movie and audio presentations.

- What do you think is more important — that the building looks good or that it is functional? Why?

9 TRANSAMERI

The Transamerica Pyramid is one of the key symbols of San Francisco. Visitors to the city cannot help but notice its 212-foot tall aluminum spire gleaming in the sunlight or sparkling at night.

This unique office tower fills up an entire city block. It was designed by William Pereira, an architect with innovative ideas. In the beginning, many residents of San Francisco were strongly opposed to the design of the Pyramid. Traditional skyscrapers were neat rectangular blocks. Critics thought the pyramid shape was too futuristic for the city. However, when the building was completed, most people were impressed by it. Today, the pyramid helps define the city of San Francisco.

---

spire: *tall narrow structure at the top of a building*
innovative: *fresh; original*

What makes a building futuristic?

ARCHITECT: William Pereira, 1909–1985

FUNCTION: Office tower

LOCATION: San Francisco, California

DATE COMPLETED: 1972

The Transamerica's pyramid shape allows sunlight to reach the streets below.

TRANSAMERICA PYRAMID

LOOKING GOOD!

The 48-story Transamerica Pyramid rises 853 feet into the air. It houses offices and shops. Two wing-like structures stick out from the 29th floor to the top of the building. These "wings" are for both form and function — they hold the elevator and stairwell.

Architect William Pereira believed that the pyramid was an ideal shape for a skyscraper as it allowed more fresh air and natural light to pass between buildings and filter down to the streets below. This helped keep the areas near the building sunlit and smog-free. Pereira's design not only followed San Francisco's shadow restriction legislation but also helped the environment.

What are the advantages and disadvantages of having a pyramid-shaped high-rise building?

Quick Fact

In 1989, the Loma Prieta earthquake (7.1 on the Richter scale) struck the Santa Cruz mountains in California. About 56 miles away, in downtown San Francisco, the Transamerica Pyramid shook for over a minute. During the quake, the top story swayed over 11 inches from side to side. Yet the building was undamaged and no one was seriously injured.

BRICKS AND MORE

The Transamerica Pyramid is built with steel, reinforced concrete, and glass. San Francisco lies in an earthquake zone. To help the building withstand strong earthquakes, engineers used shear walls in the building. Shear walls are reinforced with metal plates inside. The four-story base of the building contains about 39,370 feet of concrete and over 298 miles of steel — again, strong protection against earthquakes.

ARCHITECT

William Pereira started his career designing movie sets in Hollywood. He won three Oscars for his work! At the peak of his career in set design, he decided to focus on architecture. Pereira's designs — unique, futuristic buildings — were way ahead of the times! Pereira always considered the natural environment when designing his buildings. He once said, "It is critical to the future that we build our world without destroying the natural environment."

reinforced concrete: *strong building material made of concrete and steel bars*

Quick Fact

At the top of the building, four cameras point in the four cardinal directions. The cameras are linked to video screens in the lobby — forming a "virtual" observation deck. Visitors can have panoramic views of the city without climbing to the top of the building!

cardinal: *main (north, south, east, west)*

The Expert Says...

"The Transamerica Pyramid [is] still … a striking presence on the skyline. Its unusual design drew both praise and ridicule as it rose … nearly 40 years ago."

— Ron Evans, editor of *VIA*, a travel magazine

BUILDING by the Numbers

Check out this list of numbers to find out more cool facts about the Transamerica Pyramid.

3 The number of years it took to construct the building

18 The number of elevators inside the building

24 The number of hours it took to pour concrete into the building's foundation

48 The total number of floors in the building

50 The total number of businesses that operate inside the Transamerica Pyramid

2,025 The size of the smallest floor in square feet

21,025 The size of the largest floor in square feet

280 The total number of underground parking spaces

1,500 The approximate number of people who work in the building

1972 The year people first started occupying the building

3,678 The total number of windows

Quick Fact

It takes about a month to clean all of the windows in the Transamerica Pyramid!

Take Note

The Transamerica Pyramid stands tall at #9. Designed and built more than 20 years before the Rock and Roll Hall of Fame and Museum, it is still a unique, modern structure. Architect Pereira's design is environmentally friendly and structurally sound, offering solid protection against the area's frequent earthquakes.

- Do you think it's important for architects to take nature into account when they design their buildings? Explain.

8 HOTEL MARQ

Here's what a visitor said about this fancifully designed hotel: "You almost wouldn't mind if the bed was uncomfortable or the food cold, because just living inside such a building is a wonderful experience."

UÉS DE RISCAL

ARCHITECT: Frank O. Gehry, born 1929

FUNCTION: Hotel

LOCATION: Elciego, Spain

DATE COMPLETED: 2006

It looks like a giant gift with wild ribbons waving and gleaming in the sun — but in fact it's a hotel! Designed by architect Frank Gehry, the Hotel Marqués de Riscal (Mar-kez deh Ris-kal) really stands out from the traditional buildings of Elciego, a 150-year-old village in Spain.

The Hotel Marqués de Riscal is the first hotel designed by Gehry. Even though it looks too fanciful to be real, it is a well-planned hotel. The hotel has 43 rooms, including 11 suites. The rooms are located in two separate buildings that are joined by a suspended glass walkway. Each room features large windows that give a clear view of the vineyards and houses of Elciego. The hotel also houses a spa, a cooking school, and two restaurants.

The hotel's unusual design draws both praise and criticism. Some people call it a work of art. Others think it is a wacky misfit for the sleepy little village that surrounds it.

---

suites: *group of rooms occupied as a unit*

Do you think such a modern building belongs in an old village? Why?

HOTEL MARQUÉS DE RISCAL

LOOKING GOOD!

The most distinctive feature of this building is its colorful, wavy roof built from titanium plates. Gehry colored the titanium ribbons in shades of gold, silver, pink, and purple to match the shades of the grapes growing in the nearby vineyards. Gleaming in the sunshine, the metal ribbons are quite a sight to see. The building is raised off the ground by columns. This gives visitors a great view of the surrounding area.

BRICKS AND MORE

Frank Gehry used limestone, glass, and titanium to build this three-floor hotel. Gehry was one of the first architects to use titanium in a building. Previously, this metal had only been used to build aircraft. The titanium plates were angled in different directions to shade the windows from direct sunlight.

---

distinctive: *special; attractive*
titanium: *silvery-gray lightweight strong metal*

ARCHITECT

Architect Frank Gehry was born in Ontario, Canada. He is known for his highly unusual designs that look more like sculptures than buildings. His unique structures can be seen in many countries around the world, including the United States, Singapore, Japan, Spain, and Germany. Among his most famous buildings are the Guggenheim Museum in Bilbao, Spain, and the Walt Disney Concert Hall in Los Angeles. His designs, such as the Hotel Marqués de Riscal and the Fishdance Restaurant in Kobe, Japan, are witty, and people love them. Gehry was awarded the Pritzker Architecture Prize in 1989.

---

witty: *amusing*

A close-up of the exterior of the hotel building

Gehry's First Hotel Sparkles

A review by Susan Spano
From the *Los Angeles Times*, March 1, 2007

The theatrical, floor-to-ceiling, [deep red] drapes at the Marqués de Riscal would suit a production of … *Hamlet*.

But this is not a tragedy.

This is a guest room at the first and only hotel designed by Frank Gehry. When the curtains part at the push of a button, you see a picture window with angular contours, tilted panes, and a zigzagging window seat. The undercarriage of the roof, wrapped in pink, gold, and silver titanium ribbons, is visible in the foreground and in the distance lies the sleepy stone village of Elciego. …

The Riscal took four years to complete, partly because Gehry's Los Angeles-based architectural firm had to develop special methods for working with colored titanium. …

When [my sister and I] crested a hill, we suddenly saw the shiny ribbons of titanium — mined in Russia and Australia — draped around the roof of the hotel. Like the Guggenheim Bilbao and the Walt Disney Concert Hall in L.A., this quasi-sculptural Gehry creation could cause car crashes. It looks more like a preliminary, freehand sketch than a finished building, and it made us laugh. Gehry's buildings are like that.

---

contours: *curves*

crested: *reached the top*
quasi: *resembling in some degree*

? Why would the reviewer say that the hotel "could cause car crashes"? How would you describe the hotel in your own words?

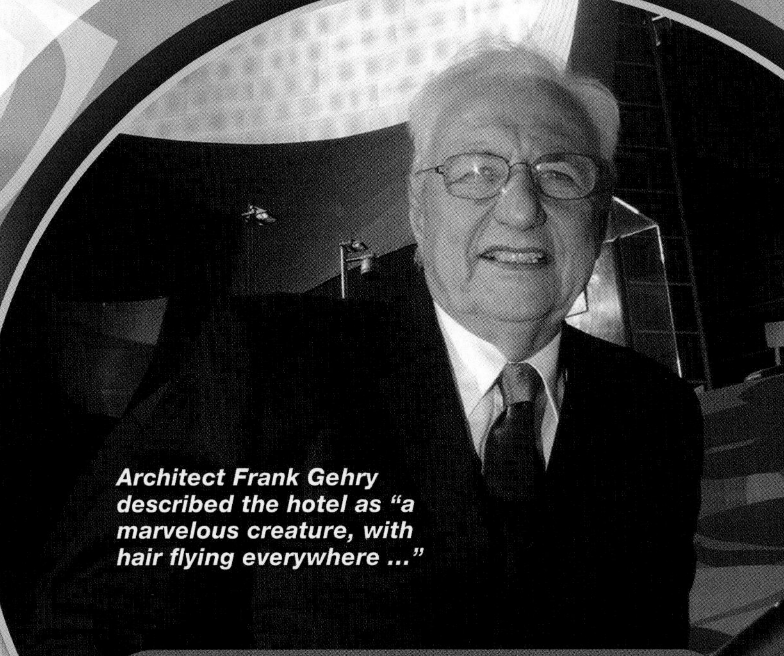

Architect Frank Gehry described the hotel as "a marvelous creature, with hair flying everywhere …"

The Expert Says …

"Thousands of … tourists pour out of coaches and cars to see this wondrous building. Gabbling in a dozen tongues, they stand awestruck amid a whirr of digital cameras."

— Jeanette Hyde, writer for *The Times*, UK

awestruck: *mesmerized*

Take Note

The Hotel Marqués de Riscal sways into the #8 spot. Gehry designed a hotel following his unique style. Engineers were able to use titanium to create the architect's unusual vision of a roof. This hotel is a work of art that makes visitors stop and stare in wonder.

- Find out more about other buildings designed by Frank Gehry. Do you agree with the statement that he is more an artist than an architect? Explain.

7 DANCING HOU

The Dancing House is a phenomenal tourist attraction in Prague.

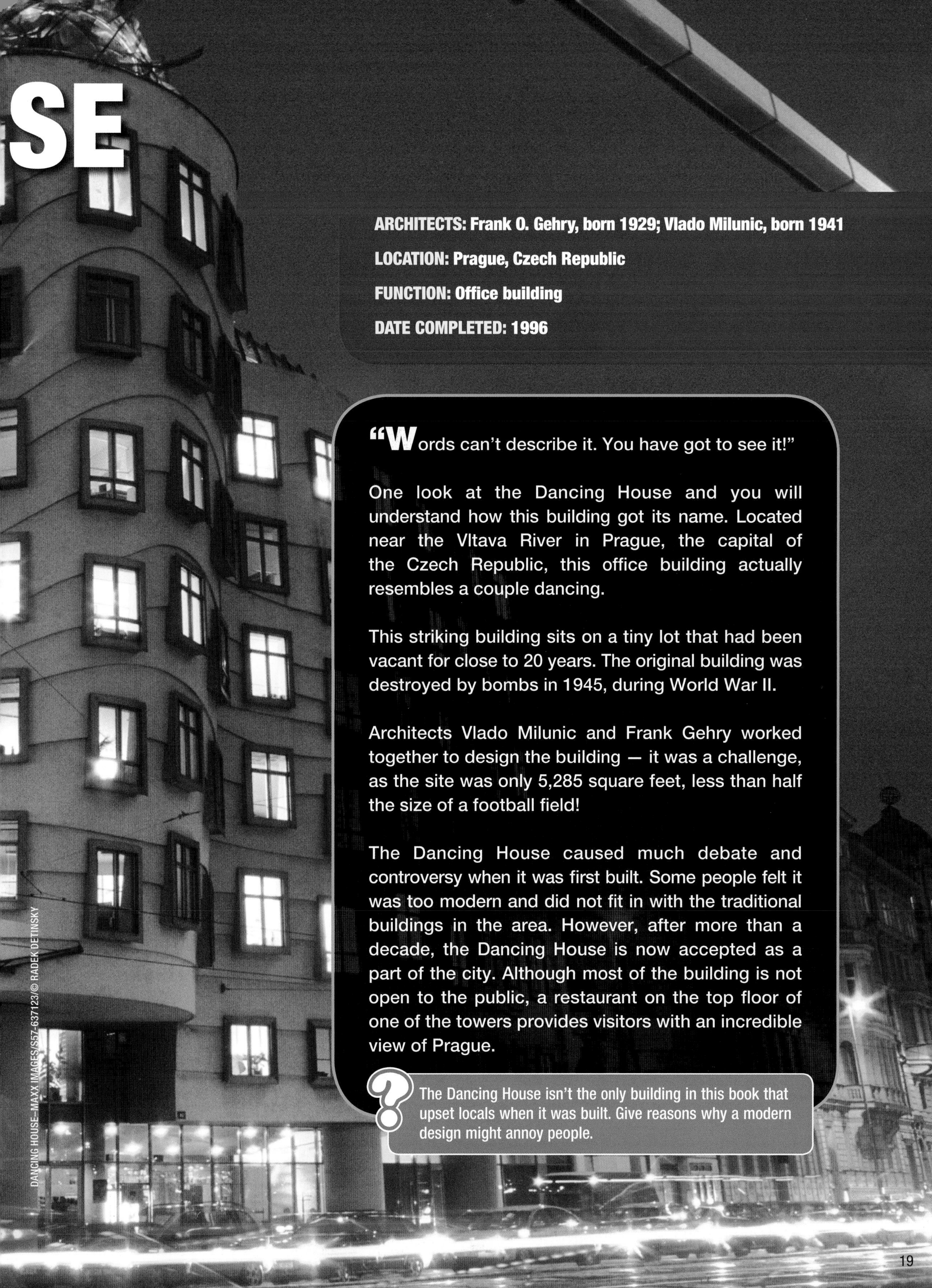

SE

ARCHITECTS: Frank O. Gehry, born 1929; Vlado Milunic, born 1941

LOCATION: Prague, Czech Republic

FUNCTION: Office building

DATE COMPLETED: 1996

"Words can't describe it. You have got to see it!"

One look at the Dancing House and you will understand how this building got its name. Located near the Vltava River in Prague, the capital of the Czech Republic, this office building actually resembles a couple dancing.

This striking building sits on a tiny lot that had been vacant for close to 20 years. The original building was destroyed by bombs in 1945, during World War II.

Architects Vlado Milunic and Frank Gehry worked together to design the building — it was a challenge, as the site was only 5,285 square feet, less than half the size of a football field!

The Dancing House caused much debate and controversy when it was first built. Some people felt it was too modern and did not fit in with the traditional buildings in the area. However, after more than a decade, the Dancing House is now accepted as a part of the city. Although most of the building is not open to the public, a restaurant on the top floor of one of the towers provides visitors with an incredible view of Prague.

? The Dancing House isn't the only building in this book that upset locals when it was built. Give reasons why a modern design might annoy people.

DANCING HOUSE

LOOKING GOOD!

The Dancing House consists of two circular towers joined together to resemble a dancing couple. The straight tower, representing the male dancer, widens near the top. The curved tower represents the female, leaning gracefully into her partner, her swaying skirt flowing out below. At the bottom of this tower, where the entrance is located, steel columns extend outward, resembling the legs of the dancer. Architect Frank Gehry nicknamed the building "Ginger and Fred," after the famous dance couple Fred Astaire and Ginger Rogers.

BRICKS AND MORE

Its unusual shape made this building a challenge to construct. Workers had to create 99 concrete panels, each one a different size and shape, for the building.

ARCHITECTS

Frank Gehry has won worldwide acclaim for his whimsical designs (see page 16). Over the years, his designs moved from conventional structures to more creative designs using unconventional materials. These buildings often resemble pieces of artistic sculptures, such as the Dancing House.

Vlado Milunic was born in Zagreb, Croatia. He has designed a total of 350 apartments, offices, and shops in Prague. For Milunic, the Dancing House represented a change from what he felt were mundane and ugly buildings constructed in the second half of the 20th century. Milunic created the orginal designs for the Dancing House. Gehry used these to continue the project.

---

whimsical: *dreamy and carefree*
mundane: *ordinary*

? Do some research. What other buildings has Vlado Milunic designed? Compare and contrast them to the Dancing House.

Quick Fact

The Dancing House stands next to a building owned by Czech playwright and former president Vaclav Havel. A strong supporter of avant garde architecture, he played a role in getting the controversial design approved and built.

avant garde: *artistically experimental*

The Expert Says...

"A structure as playful as this deserves a nickname. ... Like Fred, it has some stunning moves; like Ginger, it's a lot of fun."

— Critics from *TIME* magazine

Some Think It's HOT ... Some NOT!

The Dancing House provokes strong reactions. Here are some quotations from admirers and critics.

"The Dancing House ... is already now considered a monument, and with justice."

— Josef Stulc, president of the Czech committee for the International Council on Monuments and Sites

"[It's a] new jewel of the city's architecture ... that is adding a new aspect to its history."

— Simonetta Carbonaro, professor of Design Management, Swedish Textile School of the Borås University College

"[Gehry and Milunic] made an artistic and political statement with the [Dancing House] ... But there's also a joyful American inspiration for this tower and the solid tower it hugs ..."

— Ann Jarmusch, architecture critic for *The San Diego Union-Tribune*

"[The Dancing House] is ... perceived by many people to be an alien element. ... Some say Ginger and Fred repeats the destruction of the cityscape on this site."

— Josef Pesch, German scholar and author

" ... Wilfried Dechau, the editor of a German architectural magazine, states that the building reminds him of a 'crushed can of Coke."

— Michael Felton-O'Brien, freelance writer for *Escape From America Magazine*

"Despite its undeniable ... presence, the overall effect of [Gehry and Milunic's] ... collage is slightly disorientating."

— Helga Miklosko, writer for *The Architectural Review*

? Do you agree with people who admire this building or with those who have criticized its design? Explain.

Take Note

The Dancing House waltzes into the #7 spot. The architects made effective use of a small space and created a daring, unique structure in the midst of traditional buildings.

- Some people think the architects should have created a building that was more respectful of the fact that the original building was destroyed by wartime bombs. The architects chose to replace the building with a joyful dancing couple. Which do you think is more appropriate? Why?

LA GRANDE AR

This picture shows the Grande Arche's spectacular side walls.

CHE DE LA DÉFENSE

ARCHITECT: Johann Otto von Spreckelsen, 1929 – 1987

FUNCTION: Office tower

LOCATION: Paris, France

DATE COMPLETED: 1989

La Grande Arche de la Défense (la Grand Arsh deh la Day-fence) in Paris, France, attracts around 500,000 visitors a year. In 1982, prime minister François Mitterand launched an international competition to design a monumental piece of architecture. Mitterand wanted an architectural masterpiece to represent France's role in art, economy, and politics near the end of the 20th century. Danish architect Johann Otto von Spreckelsen's design was selected as the winner from among thousands of entries. His design of the Grande Arche was thought to represent peace and humanity rather than military triumphs. Construction began in 1982, but von Spreckelsen left the project before it was completed. Reports claim that von Spreckelsen was disappointed by his own design! After von Spreckelsen left the project, his business partner Paul Andreu took over.

Even though it looks like a giant modern monument, the Grande Arche is actually an office building. Fourteen of the country's top corporations and some government offices are located in this building. A suspended tent in the middle of the open space is used for different events such as conferences, exhibitions, and grand celebrations.

LA GRANDE ARCHE DE LA DÉFENSE–MAXX IMAGES/N99-494934/© BERNDT FISCHER

LA GRANDE ARCHE DE LA DÉFENSE

LOOKING GOOD!

This sleek building is a modern match for the many beautiful old buildings in Paris. The giant hollow cube is framed by a square arch that rises 360 feet high. The arch is 354 feet wide and 367 feet deep. It has a roof terrace that is over two acres in size. Two glass elevators take visitors to the terrace on the roof. In addition to a restaurant, the terrace offers incredible views of Paris and its suburbs.

The hollow cube in the center of the Grande Arche is large enough to hold Notre Dame de Paris — the city's famous cathedral. Architect Paul Andreu and engineer Peter Rice built a fiberglass "cloud" tent in the space. This area, known as the Espace Grande Arche, is used for different events such as exhibitions, conferences, and festive celebrations.

Espace: *French word for "open space"*

What must an architect take into consideration when designing an exhibition area?

The Expert Says...

"Megalithic, starkly white, and cubic, the soaring Grande Arche de La Défense stands as a monument ... for the French capital."

— Barry James, journalist for the *International Herald Tribune*

---

megalithic: *relating to very large stones; monumental*

BRICKS AND MORE

This amazing building has been described as a "technical and architectural feat." It was built with concrete, glass, and marble. The cloud tent inside the Arche is suspended from a web of steel cables.

ARCHITECT

Johann Otto von Spreckelsen was a Danish architect famous for designing churches in Denmark, including the Vangede Church in Copenhagen. From squares and spheres to cylinders and pyramids, von Spreckelsen consistently used simple geometrical figures in his designs. Von Spreckelsen died in 1987 and he never saw the completion of the Grande Arche.

Quick Fact

The Grande Arche resembles the famous Arc de Triomphe de l'Etoile (Arc deh Triomf deh lay-to-ahl) also located in Paris. Napoleon I ordered its construction in honor of the French army. It was built between 1806 and 1836 by architect Jean François Chalgrin.

GRANDE ARCHE

Discover more interesting facts about the Grande Arche in these FAQS (Frequently Asked Questions).

Alain Robert

Q Why does the Grande Arche look so familiar?

A This building was featured in the 2004 film *Godzilla: Final Wars*. In the film, the Grande Arche is one of the buildings damaged by Kamacuras, the monster praying mantis. This building has also made news headlines. In 1999, French building climber Alain Robert, who is physically challenged, scaled halfway up La Grande Arche de la Défense with his bare hands.

Distant view of the Grande Arche

Q How does this modern building fit with the older buildings of Paris?

A The Grande Arche sits at the end of a nearly four-mile-long axis known as the *axe historique* (historic axis) lined with historic buildings including the Louvre Museum and the Arc de Triomphe. Its simple lines are an elegant contrast to the older buildings.

View from the roof of the Grande Arche

Q How do visitors get to the roof of the Grande Arche?

A The observation platform is located on the roof of the Grande Arche. Visitors have to walk up a bank of stairs that form part of the arch's geometry. Then they travel to the roof in an outdoor glass elevator. Visitors can see the *axe historique* as they ride the elevator to the roof.

? Research the other famous buildings the Grande Arche is aligned with. Which one is the most phenomenal to you? Explain.

Take Note

The Grande Arche rises to claim the #6 spot. Its simple towers framing a giant hollow cube is unique. It gives a different feel to the city of Paris, with its many old and historic buildings. And the Grande Arche is not just a showpiece — thousands of people work here.

- Von Spreckelsen's architectural design was chosen because it represented peace and humanity. What thoughts and emotions do you have when you look at the building?

ALAIN ROBERT–AP PHOTO/MICHEL EULER; AERIAL VIEW OF THE GRANDE ARCHE–GETTY IMAGES/STONE/PASCAL CRAPET; ALL OTHER IMAGES–SHUTTERSTOCK

5 CCTV BUILDI

Imagine working inside a loop! Employees of China Central TV (CCTV), in Beijing, China, don't just imagine this type of unique workplace — they experience it every day!

Designed by Dutch architect Rem Koolhaas, the CCTV building is one seriously cool structure. No one has ever attempted to build such a daring structure before! It consists of two towers that lean toward each other — much like the Leaning Tower of Pisa, except these modern towers don't tilt by accident! The two leaning towers are connected at the top and the bottom to form a continuous loop. Quite an engineering feat!

The building's sloping external walls mean its interior spaces change in shape and size from floor to floor. This works well for the different functions for which they are used. The building houses TV production studios, communication centers, and offices.

NG

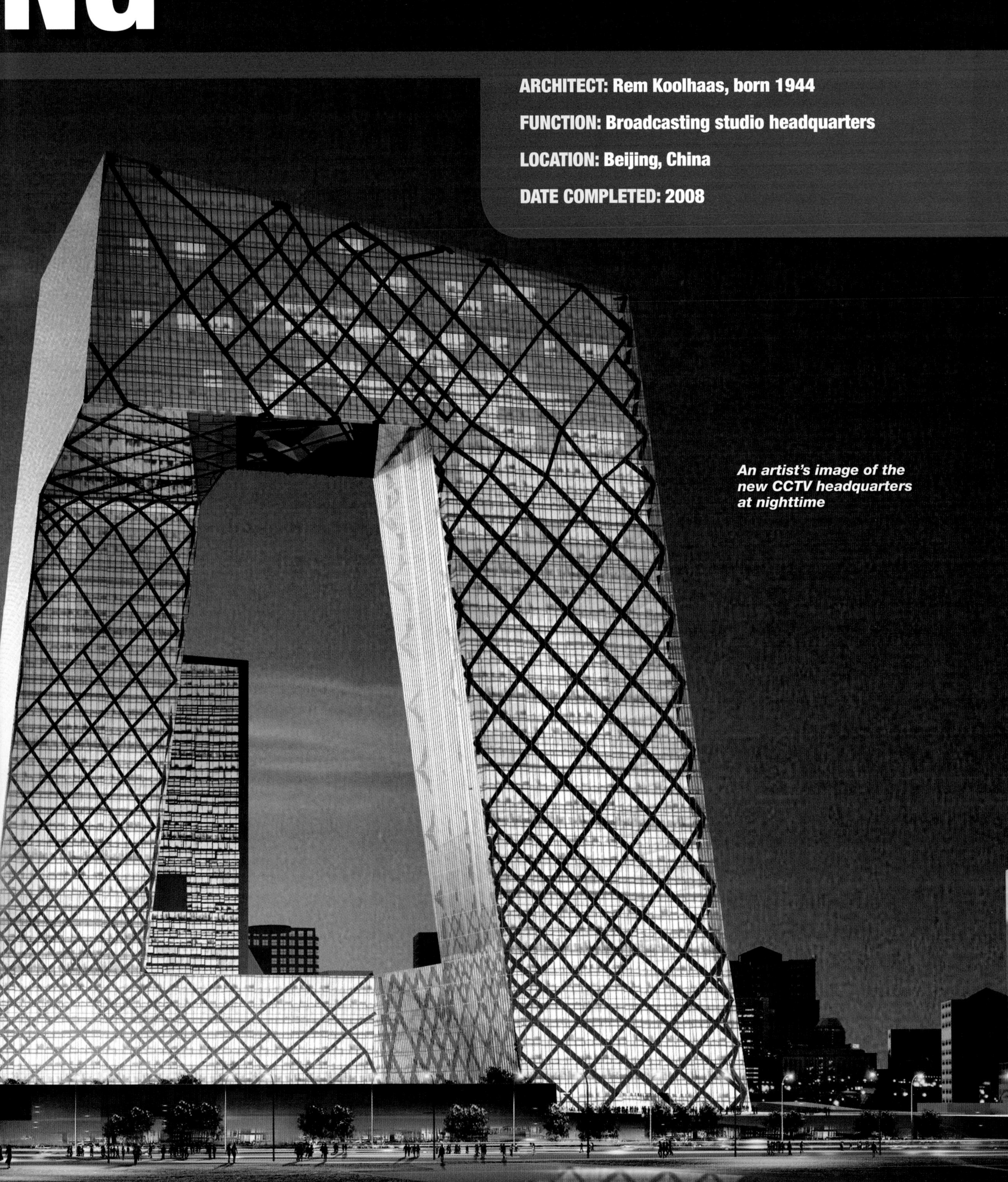

ARCHITECT: Rem Koolhaas, born 1944

FUNCTION: Broadcasting studio headquarters

LOCATION: Beijing, China

DATE COMPLETED: 2008

An artist's image of the new CCTV headquarters at nighttime

CCTV BUILDING

LOOKING GOOD!

If you see people walking near the CCTV building with their heads tilted, don't be surprised. It may mean they are having a good look at the phenomenal asymmetrical 54-story building that is changing the face of Beijing. On the ground, the two leaning towers are connected by a nine-story-high base. Up in the air, 36-stories above ground, a suspended deck links the two leaning towers. This horizontal overhang is nine to 13 stories high.

BRICKS AND MORE

The unique shape of the building breaks all of the rules in the Chinese design codes. The design had to be examined carefully by a Chinese expert review panel to make sure it was safe. Engineers then worked hard to ensure that the building is structurally solid. This is especially important as Beijing is located in a highly seismic area. The building is solidly anchored by a three-story-deep basement. It took 3,300 truckloads of concrete to build the basement of just one of the towers! The building also has a 132,000-ton steel "exoskeleton" designed to resist earthquakes.

---

asymmetrical: *irregular in shape or outline*
seismic: *prone to earthquakes*
exoskeleton: *hard outer structure*

ARCHITECT

Rem Koolhaas became famous as a journalist before he turned to architecture. His designs are very unusual. In some of his designs he has included glass floors, shimmering walls, and zigzag stairs. His goal is to blend technology with humanity. Koolhaas believes that architects can demonstrate a new vision for society in their buildings. In 2000, he won the Pritzker Prize for architecture.

? How are CCTV and the Grande Arche similar and how are they different?

Quick Fact

The CCTV building is large enough to hold 200 TV studios.

Quick Fact

Viewing holes in the floor of the suspended deck of the building will allow visitors to look directly down to the ground from almost 500 feet in the air.

The Expert Says...

"Hardly any building really engages space. Most skyscrapers exhaust space. This building leaves open the space it encapsulates. It activates the ground. It draws activities into the building."

— Ole Scheeren, architect for the Office for Metropolitan Architecture

---

encapsulates: *encloses*

The construction site of the new CCTV headquarters building, July 2007

10 9 8 7 6

BREAKING GROUND

HOW CAN TWO TOWERS BECOME ONE BUILDING? FIND OUT IN THIS STEP-BY-STEP GUIDE.

1 First, the foundation of the main building is constructed using piling rigs. Piling rigs are machines designed for drilling, impacting, and pressing piles into the ground.

2 Tower cranes are used to build the basement and a nine-story base starting from the ground up. Tower cranes are used to lift heavy materials, including steel and concrete.

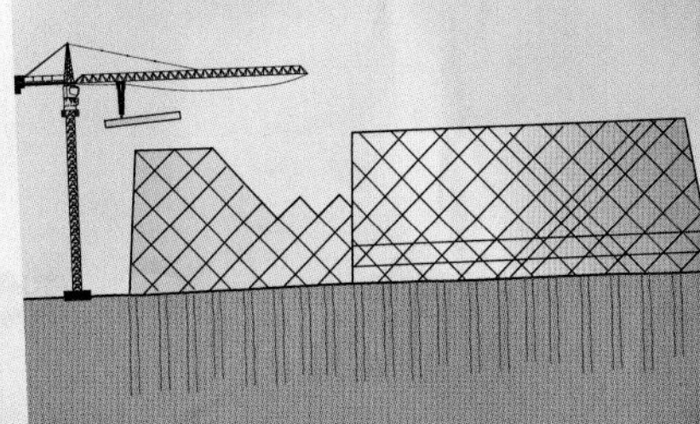

3 Next, both of the towers are constructed with two climbing cranes. Climbing cranes are placed on top of the building during construction. The cranes rise as more of the building is completed.

4 Once the tops of the towers are completed, they are used to support the construction of a two-story deck. This deck supports the overhang and links the towers together as one building.

5 Once the linking deck is completed, it creates a stable connection for the remaining floors of the building.

piles: *columns of steel or concrete driven into the ground as a foundation or support for a structure*

? Which phase of construction do you think was the most difficult and dangerous? Why?

Take Note

The CCTV building leans into the #5 spot. It took a brilliant architect to come up with the design and a team of ingenious engineers to make it possible. Its interior spaces are well designed to meet the needs of a broadcasting center.

- Some critics think architects like Rem Koolhaas try too hard to be different for no better reason than to be different. Go online and research Koolhaas's other buildings. Do you agree with the critics? Why?

5

4

CCTV BUILDING UNDER CONSTRUCTION—AP PHOTO/GREG BAKER; ALL OTHER IMAGES—SHUTTERSTOCK

4 TURIN EXHIBIT

EXHIBITION HALL– PHOTO BY NADINE RUPP/BONGARTS/GETTY IMAGES

The roof of the Turin Exhibition Hall spans 309 feet without the support of pillars.

ION HALL

ARCHITECT: Pier Luigi Nervi, 1891 – 1979

FUNCTION: Exhibition hall

LOCATION: Turin, Italy

DATE COMPLETED: 1949

At first glance, the roof of this exhibition hall looks extremely delicate. However, looks can be deceiving. The building was designed by an ingenious architect who also happened to be an engineer — and he knew how to blend strength with style.

Turin's Exhibition Hall was designed by architect-engineer Pier Luigi Nervi. His design included a huge curved roof. To build this roof, Nervi needed a material that could be shaped, that was strong, and that was lightweight. Nervi decided to build the roof using ferro-cement. This would allow him to build free and complex architectural shapes. To make ferro-cement, steel wire is coated with a thin layer of cement. It is light but strong, and can be molded into sections of any size and shape. It is prefabricated, which cuts down on cost and building time.

The Turin Exhibition Hall was completed in just eight months! It is still in use today for exhibitions and trade shows. It was even used as a hockey rink for the 2006 Winter Olympics in Italy.

---

ferro: *iron*
prefabricated: *produced ahead of time and at a different location*

TURIN EXHIBITION HALL

LOOKING GOOD!

The exhibition hall covers an area of 309 feet by 249 feet. The hall's claim to fame is its curved roof — it spans the entire building without support from beams or pillars!

An apse juts out from one end of the hall. The half-dome roof of the apse is built from the same ferro-cement as the rest of the roof.

BRICKS AND MORE

The corrugated roof was made out of ferro-cement, which is dense, but very light and flexible to work with. Using ferro-cement, Nervi was able to create a durable roof that's only about two inches thick. The roof also has many glass panels, which allow light to shine into the building.

---

apse: *semicircular projection at the front of a building or structure*
corrugated: *wavy; uneven*
dense: *having a high mass; compact*

ARCHITECT

Pier Luigi Nervi was born in the province of Sondrio in Lombardy, Italy. He was internationally known for his dramatic designs and his technical genius. He refused to let anything hold him back from creating the buildings he designed.

Ferro-cement makes it possible to eliminate the wood framework used in construction. This allows complex structures to be built with a minimum amount of materials. Nervi's buildings stand in many cities around the world, including New York City, Montreal, Sydney, and Milan.

Quick Fact

Pier Luigi Nervi designed many famous buildings other than the Turin Exhibition Hall. Nervi worked on Milan's famous Pirelli Tower. He designed Rome's Olympic Stadium and even New York City's George Washington Bridge Bus Station!

Quick Fact

Nervi always claimed that "architecture is, and must be, a synthesis of technology and art."

---

synthesis: *mixture; blend*

What do you think Nervi meant? Do you agree or disagree with him? Explain your answer.

The Expert Says...

"The series of ... structures that skyrocketed Nervi's fame began with a new exhibition hall in Turin. ... [with] one of the largest unpillared roofs in Europe."

— *TIME* magazine

The Portfolio of Pier Luigi Nervi

NERVI USED FERRO-CEMENT IN MANY OF HIS BUILDINGS, INCLUDING THOSE FEATURED IN THIS PHOTO ESSAY.

GEORGE WASHINGTON BRIDGE BUS STATION

LOCATION: New York **BUILT IN:** 1963

FYI: Who knew a simple bus station could also be an artistic masterpiece? The George Washington Bridge Bus Station stands 30 feet above the street. Angled concrete columns support the station's roof. According to ArchNewsNow.com, the roof looks as though it's "pushed and pulled like taffy."

PALAZZETTO DELLO SPORT

LOCATION: Rome, Italy **BUILT IN:** 1958

FYI: This sports stadium holds 5,000 spectators. It was built for the 1960 Rome Olympics. The Palazzetto dello Sport has a dome-shaped roof that looks very similar to the Turin Exhibition Hall. Underneath the roof are glass windows. These windows surround the whole stadium.

ST. MARY'S CATHEDRAL

LOCATION: San Francisco

BUILT IN: 1971

FYI: This 190-foot-tall masterpiece lies above visitor parking spaces. The church has a marble exterior. Stained-glass windows descend from the top to the sides of the building. Forming the walls of the building are 1,680 pre-cast pieces of concrete.

?

Besides the use of ferro-cement, how do these buildings demonstrate Nervi's creative use of concrete? Look at the photos of Nervi's buildings as you compare and contrast their designs.

Take Note

The Turin Exhibition Hall takes the #4 spot. Even though the Grande Arche and the CCTV building required a lot of skill in engineering, we feel that the Turin Exhibition Hall demonstrates more engineering innovation for its time.

- Do some research. Find out more about the role of the engineer in construction. Why was it an advantage that Nervi was both an architect and an engineer?

4

3 BIBLIOTHECA

The Bibliotheca (Bib-leo-thee-kah) Alexandrina does not look like a typical library. With its disc-like shape rising from the ground, it looks more like a futuristic spaceship! This magnificent building sits on the shores of the Mediterranean Sea. It is a celebration of a library built by the ancient Greeks on a nearby site more than 2,000 years ago.

The Bibliotheca Alexandrina is "a center for learning, tolerance, dialogue, and understanding." The library holds millions of books. It has the largest reading room in the world, with seats for 2,000! It also has a center for the Internet and its archives, and six specialized libraries. In addition, the building houses three museums, a planetarium, six art galleries, and seven research centers. And there's a conference center that can accommodate thousands of people. This is definitely no ordinary library!

Bibliotheca: *Latin word for "library"*
tolerance: *acceptance of views and traditions of others*
dialogue: *discussion*

ALEXANDRINA

ARCHITECT: The Snøhetta/Hamza Consortium

FUNCTION: Library

LOCATION: Alexandria, Egypt

DATE COMPLETED: 2002

Around 800,000 people a year visit the Bibliotheca Alexandrina.

BIBLIOTHECA ALEXANDRINA

LOOKING GOOD!

The library was designed as a tilting disc with four levels below the ground and seven levels above it. The disc design of the library represents the sun. The overall slant of the disc represents movement through time. The underground part of the building stands for the past, the ground level represents the present, and the levels above the ground symbolize the future. The ground level marks the point at which the present meets the past and future.

? Compare the setting and design of the Hotel Marqués de Riscal and the Bibliotheca Alexandrina. What are some of the similarities and differences?

BRICKS AND MORE

The Bibliotheca Alexandrina's outside circular wall is covered in 4,000 granite blocks. These blocks are carved with the letters of alphabets from around the world. The circular wall is considered the largest in the world, with a diameter of 525 feet and a height of 115 feet. The architecture and technology of the building are considered groundbreaking. Glazed panels on the roof let natural light into the building. Engineers used computers to calculate the position of the roof panels — the panels tilt at an angle that lets in the most light with the least amount of direct sunlight.

ARCHITECT

Craig Dykers is the principal designer of the Snøhetta/Hamza Consortium, which designed the building. At the start of his career as an architect, he learned of the competition to design the Bibliotheca Alexandrina. He quickly put together a team of young architects from around the world — and they won the competition! Dykers believes in collaboration in design. He said, "Buildings are used by many people, and many people should have input into how they are created."

collaboration: *several people working together*

? The Snøhetta/Hamza Consortium worked as a team. Do you think this is better than one architect working alone on a project? Why?

Exterior circular wall

Quick Fact

The library's Internet archive keeps a copy of all web pages on every Web site since 1996. It is the second such archive in the world — the first one is in San Francisco, California.

The reading room

The Expert Says...

"... The Bibliotheca Alexandrina experience was and still is quite reminiscent for everyone ... [and it devised] new criteria for the reasoning of such buildings."

— Heba Safey Eldeen, writer for *Architecture Plus Magazine*

reminiscent: *reminding someone of something else*

Egypt Opens New LIBRARY OF ALEXANDRIA

A REPORT BY CHAD COHEN
FROM *NATIONAL GEOGRAPHIC TODAY*, OCTOBER 16, 2002

... Alexandria is trying to recapture the spirit of perhaps its richest legacy — the Great Library of Alexandria — by opening the new Bibliotheca Alexandrina. ...

"In a world worried about the clash of civilizations, about war, ... I think it's significant that out of Egypt comes this new library, a place of understanding, learning, tolerance, and brotherhood," said Ismail Serageldin, the library's director. ...

During the 1980s, Egypt and the United Nations Educational, Scientific and Cultural Organization [UNESCO] resolved to build the Bibliotheca Alexandrina with the same universal goals as the ancient one: a focal point for research, the advancement of knowledge, and the open exchange of ideas. ...

Countries from around the world contributed to the $220 million-plus building effort. ...

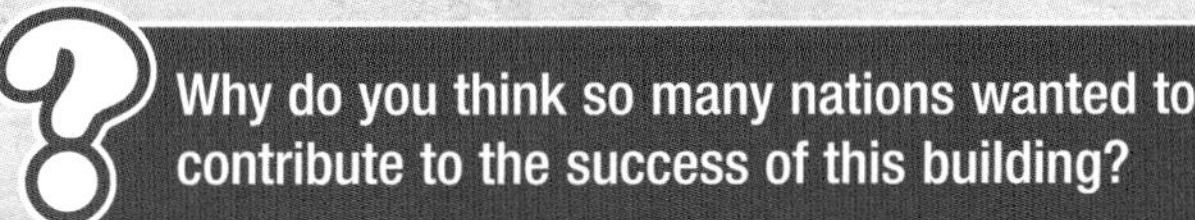

Why do you think so many nations wanted to contribute to the success of this building?

The first and most famous blow to the ancient library came in 48 B.C., when Julius Caesar laid siege to Alexandria and set fire to the city. Historians believe flames consumed about 10 percent of the library.

By midpoint in the new millennium, the library had fallen completely. Historians believe that not a single scroll survives.

Today the new Bibliotheca Alexandrina proves that perhaps the most important element of the ancient library persists — its spirit. And this time the building is fireproof.

legacy: *something received from the past*
focal point: *center of activity*

This is an artistic image of the Great Library of Alexandria.

The slope of the Bibliotheca Alexandrina's roof gives the impression that part of the building is underwater.

Take Note

The Bibliotheca Alexandrina sweeps into the #3 spot. It has one of the most innovative designs and the building serves many important functions: as a library, museum, planetarium, and research center. It is a cultural link that reaches back to ancient history and forward to the technological age.

- Some critics feel that the design of the library should have reflected the character of the neighborhood, which consists of traditional buildings. Do you agree? Explain.

2 SYDNEY OPE

SYDNEY OPERA HOUSE—SHUTTERSTOCK

Architect Jorn Utzon's futuristic design for the Sydney Opera House took 16 years to build.

RA HOUSE

ARCHITECT: Jorn Utzon, born 1918

FUNCTION: Performing arts center

LOCATION: Sydney, Australia

DATE COMPLETED: 1973

The Sydney Opera House put Sydney, Australia, on the cultural map. Completed over 30 years ago, this remarkable building is still considered a masterpiece.

The Sydney Opera House stands on Bennelong Point, a narrow piece of land that juts out into Sydney Harbour. It consists of three shell-shaped structures that house 1,000 rooms — including concert halls, lounges, restaurants, and dressing rooms. The roof is an architectural wonder. When architect Jorn Utzon first conceived of the design in 1957, he was far ahead of his time. No one had the engineering ability to build the roof he had envisioned! It took years of collaboration between Utzon and engineer Ove Arup to finally work out how to create the roof.

Today, the Opera House is one of the busiest performing arts centers in the world. Each year, it offers 3,000 events on its stages, with two million people in attendance! The building not only has a dazzling form, it brilliantly serves the purpose for which it was built!

As architect Frank O. Gehry wrote in *The Atlantic*, November 2007: "Real architecture tends to have an uplifting effect on the people that experience it, and it creates identifiable icons — like the Sydney Opera House — that brands a city, even a country."

Think about the Statue of Liberty and the Eiffel Tower. Would you say that they brand the U.S. and France? Why or why not?

SYDNEY OPERA HOUSE

LOOKING GOOD!

The most outstanding feature of the Opera House is its roof. For years, people have compared the unique roof to the billowing sails of boats. In a 1992 interview with Australia's *Good Weekend* magazine, architect Jorn Utzon said, "Many people say my design was inspired by the sailing yachts in the harbor or by seashells. This is not the case. It is like an orange, you peel an orange and you get these segments, these similar shapes. It was like this in my models."

What does the roof make you think of — sails or orange segments?

BRICKS AND MORE

Engineer Ove Arup described the building of the Sydney Opera House as "an adventure into the unknown." Utzon worked closely with Arup and engineers around the world to create the prefabricated concrete sections for the roof. It took 16 years to complete the building. The engineers were pushed to the limits of their ability. This iconic 20th-century building cost more than $90 million to complete!

---

billowing: *bulging, swelling out*

ARCHITECT

Danish architect Jorn Utzon's cutting-edge design was the winner of an international competition to design the Sydney Opera House. During the long process of building the unique structure, tension rose between Utzon and the state government over delays and rising costs. In 1966, Utzon resigned from the project in frustration. Architect Peter Hall took over the project and completed the building in 1973.

Utzon went on to a very successful career building public buildings and housing projects. In 2003, he was awarded the Pritzker Prize for Architecture.

Quick Fact

On October 20, 1973, the Sydney Opera House was officially opened by Queen Elizabeth II.

The Expert Says...

"None of Utzon's other buildings — churches, government departments, houses — looks anything like [the Sydney Opera House.] ... Architects today who try to copy his concept always end up looking very second-rate indeed."

— Hugh Pearman, architecture and design critic for *The Sunday Times*, London, UK

Quick Fact

The roof of the opera house is built of ferro-cement, the same material used in the Turin Exhibition Hall.

In 2004, the Reception Hall at the Sydney Opera House was renovated using Utzon's original design. Renamed the Utzon room, it is the only interior space in the opera house designed by the architect.

Sydney Opera House

Check out this list of numbers showing the materials used in the construction of this site.

In 2007, the Sydney Opera House was proclaimed a United Nations World Heritage Site. In making the announcement, the committee said this artistic monument "has had an enduring influence on the ... architecture of the late 20th century."

2,194 precast concrete sections, each weighing close to 16.5 tons, make up the roof

Over one million tiles cover the roof

400 miles of electric cable run throughout the building

67,005 square feet of glass used in the building

217 miles of tensioned steel cable hold the roof sections together

Quick Fact

The tallest area of the curved roof is around 220 feet above the sea. The opera house rests on concrete piers sunk as far as 82 feet below sea level!

Take Note

The Sydney Opera House takes the #2 spot. This unique structure brought together a visionary architect with a cutting-edge design, and a talented engineering team that pushed their skills to the limit. This building efficiently houses one of the leading performing arts centers of the world.

- Jorn Utzon, creator of the project, left before the Sydney Opera House was completed. Did that affect the final outcome in any way? Explain.

UTZON ROOM—COURTESY OF SYDNEY OPERA HOUSE TRUST; ALL OTHER IMAGES—SHUTTERSTOCK, ISTOCKPHOTO

1 GUGGENHE

"I need a fighter, a lover of space, an agitator, a tester and a wise man ... I want a temple of spirit, a monument!"

Those were the words that Hilla Rebay, art adviser to Solomon R. Guggenheim, sent to architect Frank Lloyd Wright. Rebay was asking Wright to design a museum to display Guggenheim's collection of non-objective paintings (paintings that contain no recognizable figures or objects).

Frank Lloyd Wright came through. This "wise man" and "lover of space" designed a museum that offers visitors an incredible, light-filled space in which to view the art. The "fighter," "agitator," and "tester" took 13 years to design and build the innovative museum. He made over 700 different sketches before the owners and the city of New York were happy with the design!

The Guggenheim Museum is unlike any other museum. At the time it was built, most buildings were in the shape of boxes or rectangular prisms. The Guggenheim shocked people with its blend of shapes and rounded walls. Wright created a building made up of what has been described as "a symphony of triangles, ovals, arcs, and squares."

The Guggenheim is one of Frank Wright's most important buildings. He died just five weeks before the building was completed. More than 40 years later, no other building can compete with the Guggenheim for its winning form and function.

---

agitator: *person who stirs up discussion or opposition*

5 AV
MUSEUM MILE

GUGGENHEIM MUSEUM–GETTY IMAGES/STONE/JOHN LAMB

IM MUSEUM

ARCHITECT: Frank Lloyd Wright, 1867–1959

FUNCTION: Museum

LOCATION: New York City, New York

DATE COMPLETED: 1959

Around 16,000 people visited the Guggenheim Museum on the day it opened.

GUGGENHEIM MUSEUM

Quick Fact

The Guggenheim Museum in New York is part of a series of international museums that are run by the Solomon R. Guggenheim Foundation.

LOOKING GOOD!

Wright created an upside down ziggurat for the museum. Its free-flowing open spaces are very different from traditional museums with their linked square rooms. At the Guggenheim, visitors step into an elevator that takes them to the top of the building. Then they stroll down the circular ramp, which is wrapped around a huge open rotunda. As they wind their way down, visitors can view the art in self-contained sections running off the ramp. The open rotunda also makes it possible for visitors to see several sections of artwork on different levels at the same time.

---

ziggurat: *ancient pyramidal structure with staircases on the outside*
rotunda: *round room or building, usually domed*

The Sydney Opera House took 16 years to design and build. The Guggenheim Museum took 13 years. Why do you think it took so long to build them?

BRICKS AND MORE

Frank Lloyd Wright chose gunite (guhn-ahyt), a mixture of cement, sand, and water, to create the curved exterior walls of the museum. According to the *New York Times*, workers sprayed gunite "into a plywood framework reinforced with steel."

In order to get smooth rounded exterior walls, Wright chose not to use expansion joints. These joints prevent cracks by making it possible for the walls to expand and contract in different weather conditions. As a result, cracks have formed in the walls of the museum. In the 1990s, repairs were done to fix the problem.

ARCHITECT

In a career that spanned 70 years, architect Frank Lloyd Wright designed and built over 500 buildings. A lover of nature, he coined the term "organic architecture" to describe designs inspired by nature. Wright had a huge influence on architecture with his concept of open floor plans and exterior designs that blended with the environment.

Quick Fact

It cost more than $3 million to build the Guggenheim Museum.

Visitors to the Guggenheim follow this spiraling ramp while admiring some of the world's most significant artwork.

Through the GRAPEVINE

CHECK OUT THESE QUOTES TO SEE WHAT MAKES THE GUGGENHEIM MUSEUM AN EYE-POPPING EXPERIENCE.

"Entering into the spirit of this interior, you will discover the best possible atmosphere in which to show fine paintings or listen to music. It is this atmosphere that seems to me most lacking in our art galleries, museums, music halls and theaters."

— **FRANK LLOYD WRIGHT**

Why is atmosphere an important thing to consider when creating a building? Do you think museum buildings lack atmosphere? Explain.

The museum's glass dome is almost 92 feet above the ground. It lights up the whole building. The dome is made out of Pyrex, a type of glass that resists heat.

"... I can run through the Guggenheim very quickly and I [can] come down and I see the same things again differently. So I see [artwork] from every different perspective."

— **ZAHA HADID, ARCHITECT**

"The paintings project from the wall on long metal arms attached to the centers of their backs, seeming to float in space ... They are thus beautifully revealed, but at the expense of the total architectural harmony."

— ***THE NEW YORK TIMES***

According to New York magazine, the Guggenheim Museum "is designed like a nautilus shell so you can see art from multiple levels."

nautilus: mollusk with a spiral chambered shell

The Expert Says...

"Wright produced a vibrant building whose architecture is as refreshing now as it was 40 years ago."

— Matthew Drutt, Associate Curator for Research, Guggenheim Museum, New York

Take Note

The Guggenheim Museum takes the #1 spot. Frank Lloyd Wright's groundbreaking design plays on curves and light. The winding ramp invites visitors to stroll through the museum and view everything it has to offer. All this combined makes this building a thing of beauty and functionality.

- Frank Lloyd Wright was one of the most important architects of modern times. Find out more about how his designs influenced and shaped the homes and buildings of the 20th century.

We Thought ...

Here are the criteria we used in ranking the 10 most phenomenal modern buildings.

The building:

- Features beautiful or innovative design
- Effectively uses interior space
- Was built using efficient and creative materials
- Uses building materials in an exceptional way
- Has multiple functions
- Has become an icon
- Evokes strong reactions in people
- Continues to attract many visitors

What Do You Think?

1. Do you agree with our ranking? If you don't, try ranking these buildings yourself. Justify your ranking with data from your own research and reasoning. You may refer to our criteria, or you may want to draw up your own list of criteria.

2. Here are three other buildings we considered but in the end did not include in our top 10 list: the pyramid of the Louvre Museum, the Palazzetto dello Sport, and the Walt Disney Concert Hall.
   - Find out more about these buildings. Do you think they should have made our list? Give reasons for your response.
   - Are there other buildings that you think should have made our list? Explain your choices.

Index